Most mammals are wary of humans and are difficult to observe in the field. However, their presence can be detected by the signs (clues) they leave behind as they move from place to place. Signs include any disturbance or change to a natural environment, ranging from a blade of nibbled grass, to a track in the mud, to a hole in the ground.

Knowing what to look for and how to differentiate signs makes detection relatively simple.

- The best times of day for tracking are dawn and dusk when many animals are most active in leaving or returning to their nests and dens. Seasonally, spring and early summer will most likely offer the most tracks as this is when many species are active throughout the day.

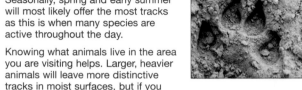

- Knowing what animals live in the area you are visiting helps. Larger, heavier animals will leave more distinctive tracks in moist surfaces, but if you are looking in the right place, at the right time of day, you'll see bird and small-to-medium animal tracks as well.

- The key signs to look for include tracks and trails, droppings, feeding signs and dens, burrows or nesting sites. Tracks are most easily seen in mud or sand, so look along muddy trails, on lake shores or riverbanks and along beaches while you hone your skills.

Wildlife Watching Etiquette

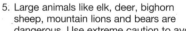

1. Honor the rights of private landowners and other wildlife viewers.

2. Leave pets at home.

3. Give animals room to move and act naturally.

4. Never touch orphaned or sick animals or try to feed wildlife; they can transmit deadly diseases like Hanta Virus via contact or by inhaling the virus. Contact Texas Parks & Wildlife (TPWD) if you find an animal injured or in distress.

5. Large animals like elk, deer, bighorn sheep, mountain lions and bears are dangerous. Use extreme caution to avoid attracting their attention.

6. Report any encounters with dangerous animals.

Made in the USA

Waterford Press publishes reference guides that introduce readers to nature observation, outdoor recreation and survival skills. Product information is featured on the website: www.waterfordpress.com

ISBN 978-1-62005-565-6

$7.95 U.S.

5 0 7 9 5

9 781620 055656

UPC

8 84682 01482 7

10 9 8 7 6 5 4 3 2 1   2202801

T0123972

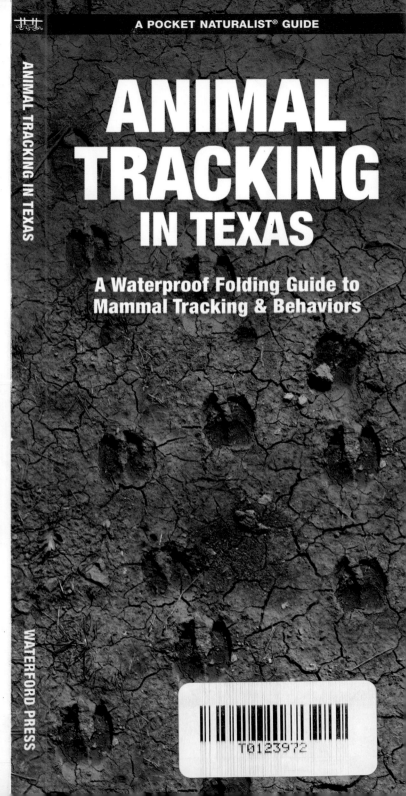

ANIMAL TRACKING IN TEXAS

ANIMAL TRACKING IN TEXAS

A Waterproof Folding Guide to Mammal Tracking & Behaviors

WATERFORD PRESS

DROPPINGS

The size, shape, color and content of droppings (scat) give key information about the animal and its diet. In general, the scat of predators are long and twisted and contain the fur, feathers or bones of its prey. Herbivores have pellet-like or pie-like scat depending on their diet and the time of year.

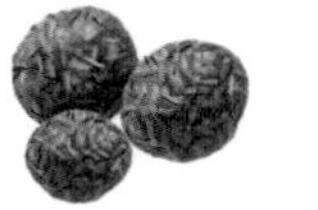

Rabbits & Hares
Distinctive round scat is about .5 in. (1.3 cm) long.

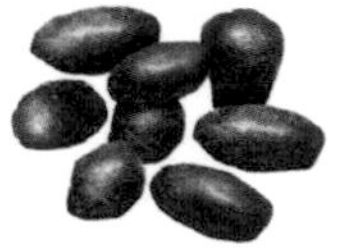

Squirrel
Cylindrical pellets are about .5 in. (1.3 cm) long.

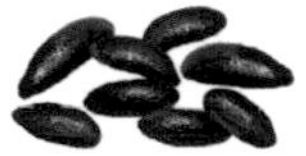

Mice & Rats
Cylindrical, rice-like scat is between .3 in. and .8 in. (.8-2 cm) long.

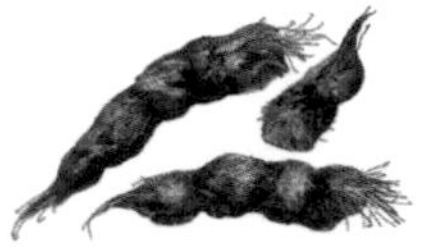

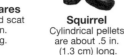

Dog Family
Scat is usually a single cord with a pointed end. Droppings vary greatly in size and diameter and may be up to 5 in. (13 cm) long.

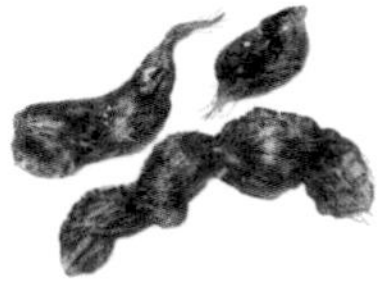

Porcupine
Pellets are about 1 in. (3 cm) long and often collect in huge piles in and around their dens and under trees.

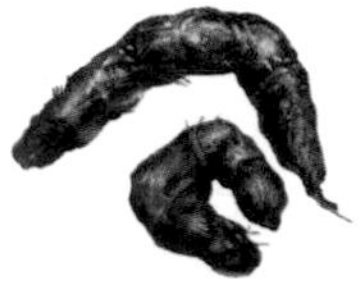

Weasel Family
Scat is usually black and twisted and may be up to 4 in. (10 cm) long. Family members include weasels, minks, skunks, otters and badgers.

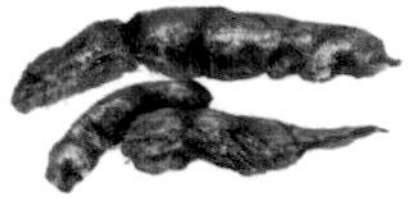

Cat Family
Scat is usually segmented and often buried. It varies in size and may be up to 4 in. (10 cm) long.

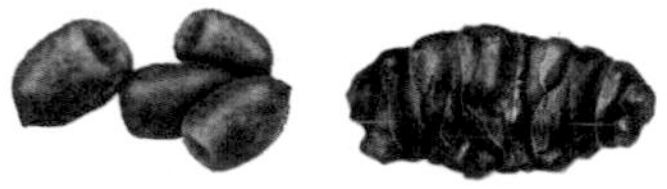

Deer Family
Distinctive pellet scat is pointed on one end and concave on the other. Scat varies in shape, but is about 1 in. (3 cm) long and deposited in small piles. Droppings are typically pellets in winter and chips or "pies" in summer. Family members include deer, pronghorns, elk, mountain goats, caribou and bighorn sheep.

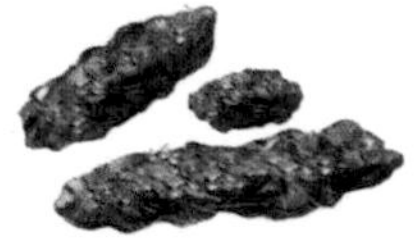

Northern River Otter
Scat is up to 7 in. (18 cm) long and .75 in. (2 cm) in diameter. Black when fresh, it is often deposited in piles in conspicuous places along the water's edge.

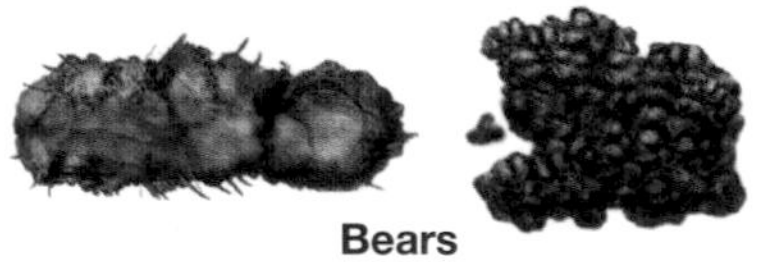

Bears
Scat is typically thick (to 2 in./ 5 cm wide) and cord-like, with blunt ends. When bears eat primarily vegetation, e.g., during the autumn berry season, scat forms a loose mass, like a cow patty.

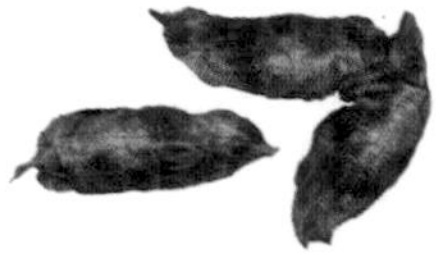

Nutria
Droppings are dark green or black, about 2 in. (5 cm) long and .5 in. (1.3 cm) in diameter, with deep parallel grooves along the side. Often found near rivers, streams or ponds.

TIP If you find scat with berries or a distinguishable food source in it, locate the food source to find additional animal signs.

FEEDING SIGNS

Look for teeth marks on plants, nuts and bones. Bears will often tear up the earth or roll logs in search of insects or rodents. Owls cough up fuzzy pellets of the fur and bones of rodents.

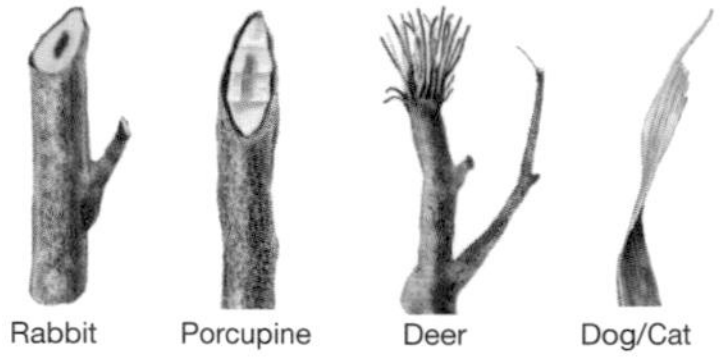

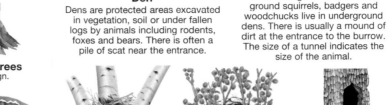

Browse
The browsed ends of twigs can indicate who ate them. Rabbits slice off the ends of twigs cleanly at a 45-degree angle. Porcupines leave rows of small bite marks on twig ends. Deer and moose break the ends off twigs and cause the tips to fray. Cats and dogs raggedly chew off the tops of grasses.

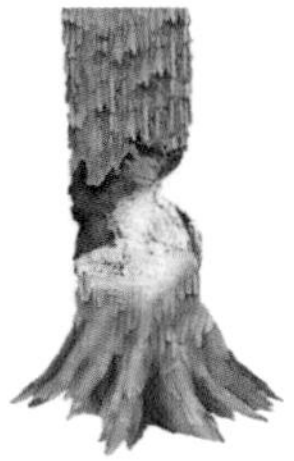

Gnawed Trees
Beaver sign.

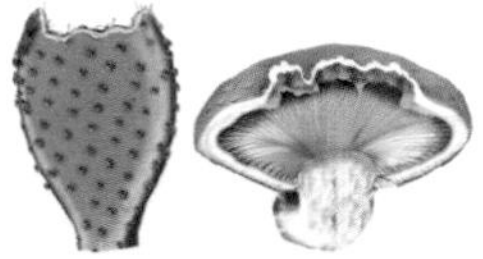

Chewed Plants
Rodent or deer sign.

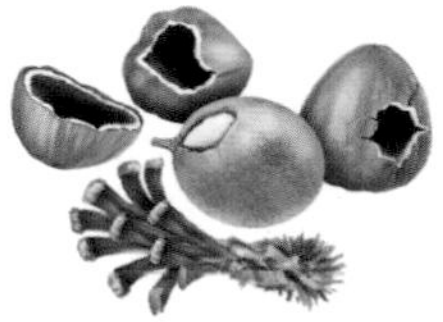

Chewed Nuts and Stripped Cones
Hollowed nuts and stripped cones indicate the presence of rodents like squirrels, chipmunks and mice, and birds such as nuthatches, crossbills and woodpeckers.

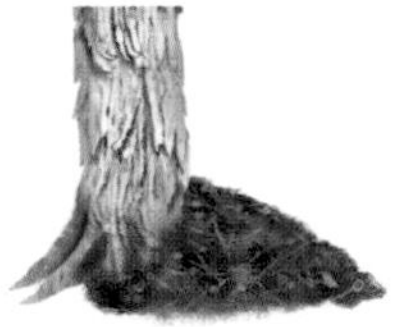

Squirrel Midden
A large pile of cone, nut and plant litter can be found beneath a favorite feeding spot, often at the base of a tree.

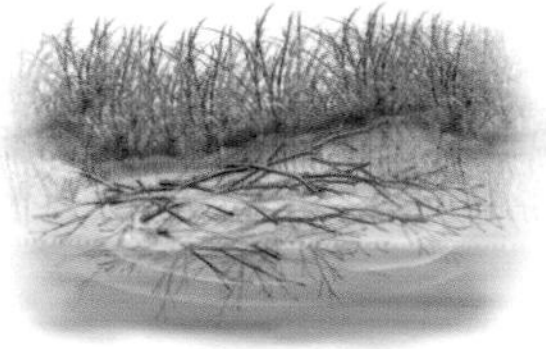

Beaver Sign
Beavers will stack branches in shallow water when preparing their food supply for winter.

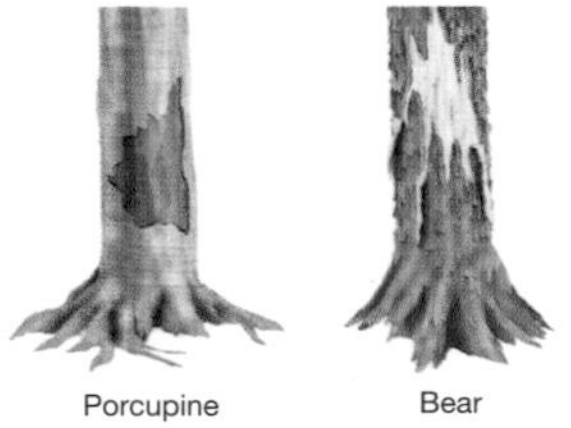

Barked Trees
Porcupines, beavers and hoofed mammals will chew off large patches of tree bark. Bears often tear the bark off the lower trunk to feed on sap.

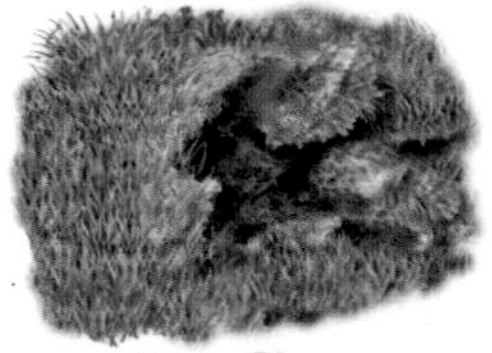

Bear Sign
Bears tear up large patches of earth while digging up roots and rodents.

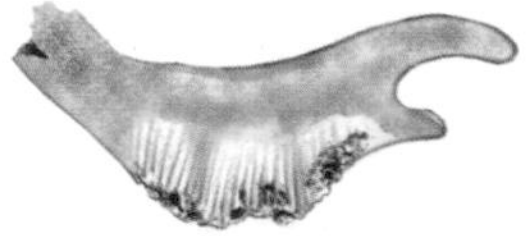

Gnawed Bones
Mice, squirrels and other rodents leave teeth marks on the bones of dead animals.

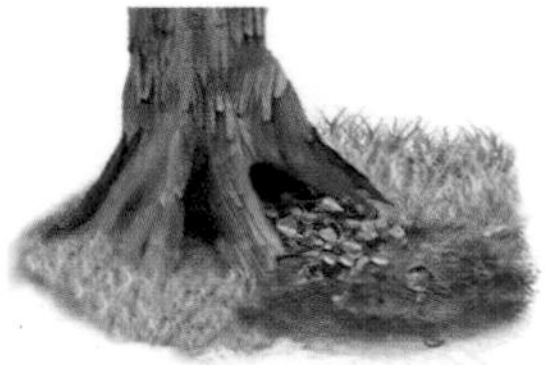

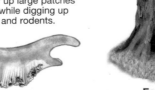

Food Cache
Squirrels, chipmunks and mice often cache food in protected areas for the winter.

NESTING SITES

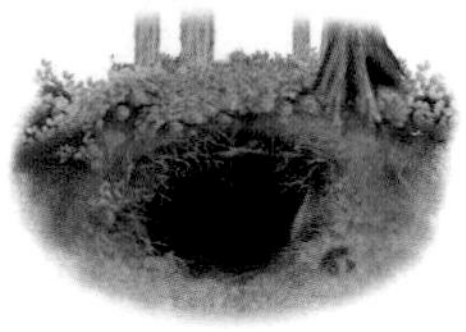

Den
Dens are protected areas excavated in vegetation, soil or under fallen logs by animals including rodents, foxes and bears. There is often a pile of scat near the entrance.

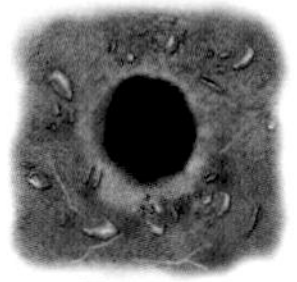

Burrow
A wide range of rodents from ground squirrels, badgers and woodchucks live in underground dens. There is usually a mound of dirt at the entrance to the burrow. The size of a tunnel indicates the size of the animal.

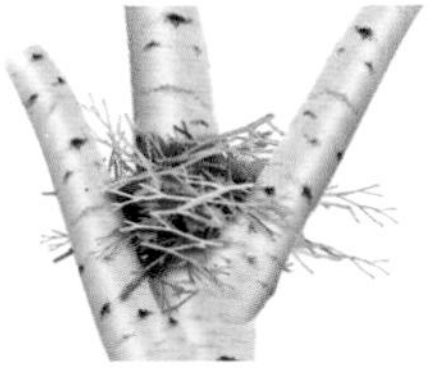

Squirrel Nest
Rounded nests of leaves and twigs are often located in a crotch of tree branches.

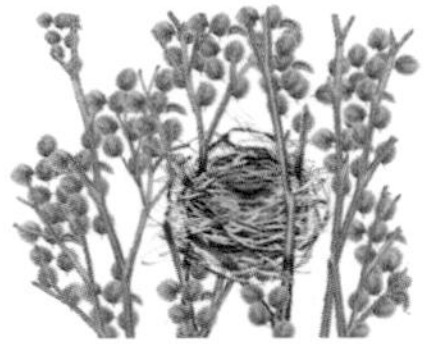

Mouse Nest
Rounded nests are made of grasses and are often located above the ground in the branches of shrubs.

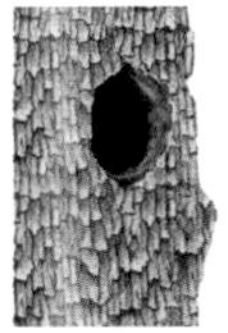

Tree Hole
Usually drilled by woodpeckers, it can be home to a variety of creatures.

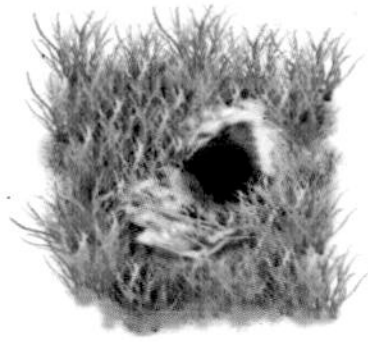

Rabbit Nest
Rabbits create slight depressions in the earth and use grasses and their fur to line the nest and create a lid to cover it.

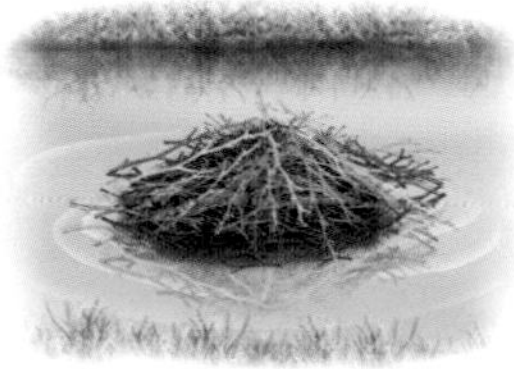

Beaver Lodge
Lodge is located in the middle of a pond and is constructed primarily of sticks and mud. Size is variable, but is typically over 4 ft. (1.2 m) high and 10 ft. (3 m) in diameter.

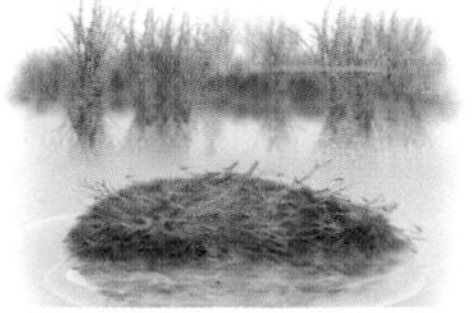

Muskrat Lodge
Dome-shaped lodge is constructed of marsh plants and mud. Size is variable, but it is typically over 2 ft. (60 cm) high and 3 ft. (90 cm) in diameter.

OTHER SIGNS

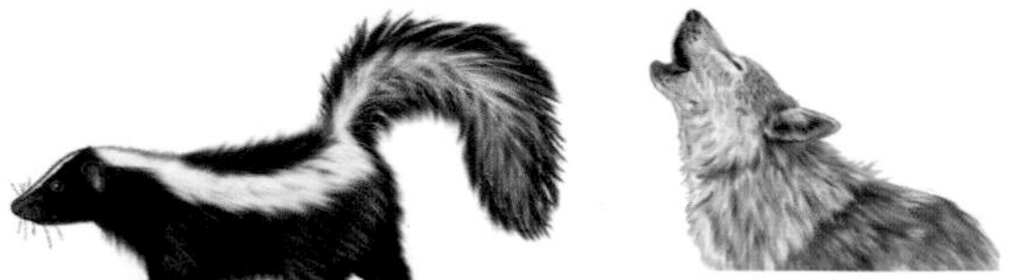

Smells
Many animals like skunks, weasels and foxes have distinctive smells. Bears smell like rotting garbage. Wolves, deer and mountain lions often mark their territory by depositing scat or spraying fetid urine on objects.

Sounds
Wolves and coyotes howl, elk bugle, rabbits and hares thump their back feet on the ground when they sense danger, and beavers slap their tails on the water before diving for the same reason. Marmots and prairie dogs whistle loudly when danger approaches.

OTHER SIGNS

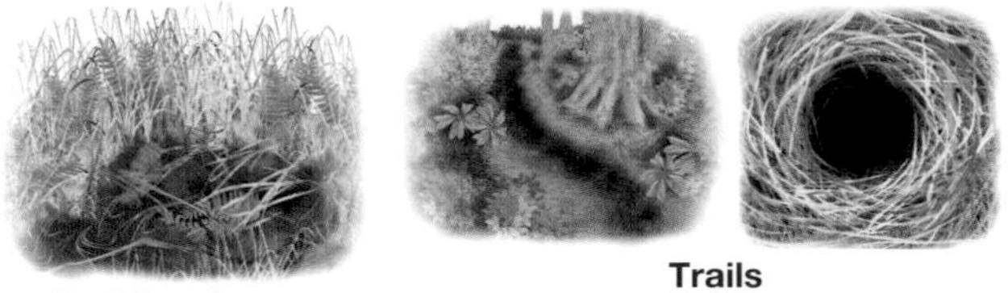

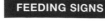

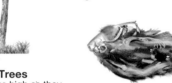

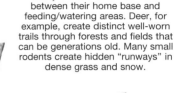

Bedding Areas
Deer and other hoofed mammals create oval areas of matted vegetation where they sleep.

Trails
Many animals establish trails between their home base and feeding/watering areas. Deer, for example, create distinct well-worn trails through forests and fields that can be generations old. Many small rodents create hidden "runways" in dense grass and snow.

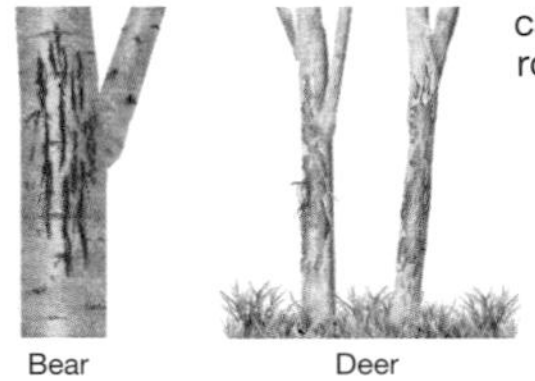

Scratch Marks on Trees
Bears will claw and bite trees as high as they can reach. Bobcats sometimes use trees as scratching posts. Rodents and raccoons leave scratch marks on trees while climbing. Male deer will often rub the bark off the lower extremities of smaller trees with their antlers.

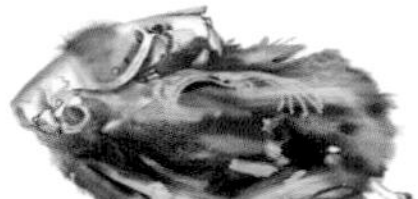

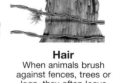

Bird Pellet
Owls, eagles, hawks, ravens and gulls are a few species of birds that commonly regurgitate pellets comprised of undigestible material. The pellets superficially resemble animal scat, but are comprised of hair, feathers and bones.

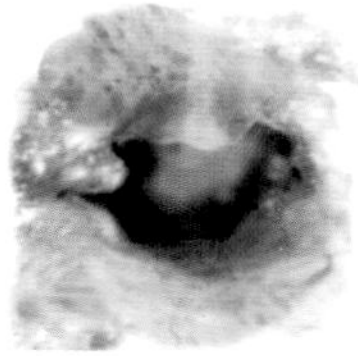

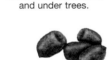

Breathing
In cold weather, resting/ hibernating mammals can be detected by the white breath they exhale from their resting place.

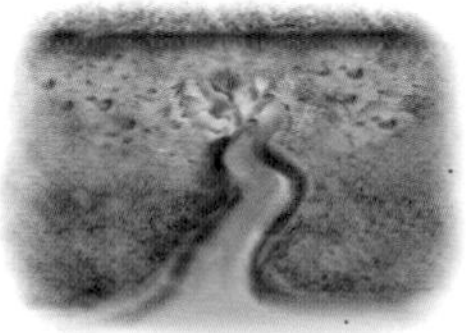

Slides
River otters often create "slides" on the banks of ponds or rivers that they use when entering the water.

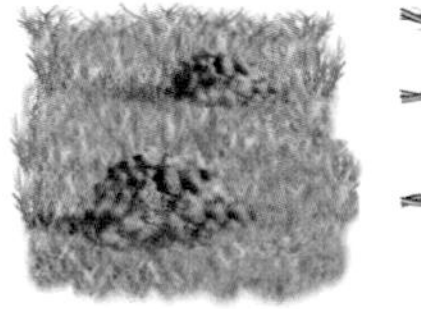

Mounds
Moles and pocket gophers rarely surface, but their presence can be detected by the mounds of earth they push up while tunneling.

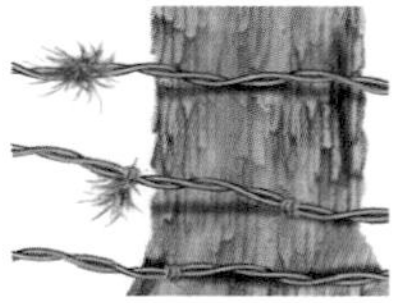

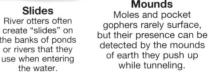

Hair
When animals brush against fences, trees or logs, they often leave behind tufts of hair. Look for tracks in the area to decipher who the hair belongs to.

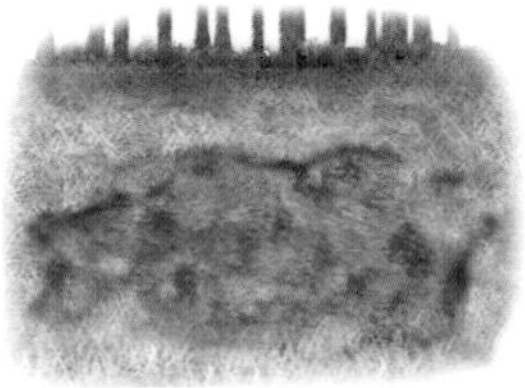

Scraped Depression/Wallow
During mating season, male elk and deer will paw the vegetation off an area of earth and mark the site with urine or feces.

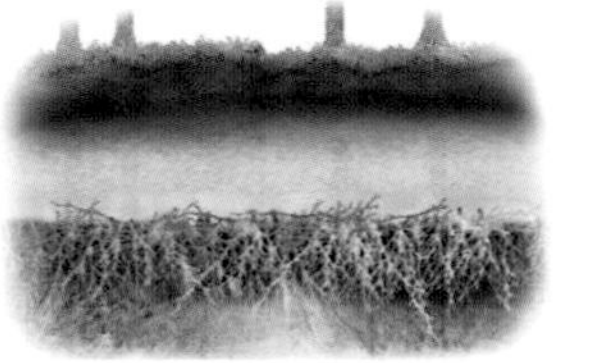

Beaver Dam
Beavers create a linear pile of logs at right angles to the water flow in order to create a pond in which to build their lodge. It can be several feet high and up to 100 yds. (91 m) long.

Porcupine

Hind tracks are 3-4 in. (8-10 cm) long. Note straight toes. Claws are prominent. An ambler, it walks with its front foot and same side back foot moving at the same time. Leaves piles of droppings at tree base. Chews large patches of bark off trees. Smells like chicken soup.

Armadillo

Distinctive tracks have 5 toes on the hind foot and 4 on the front foot and are 1-2 in. (3-5 cm) long. Claws are prominent. Tracks in soft soil usually show tail drag between feet.

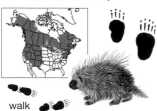

walk

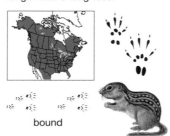

walk

Squirrels/Chipmunks

Hind tracks are 1-2 in. (3-5 cm) long with 5 toes. Front tracks are smaller and show 4 toes.

Ground Squirrels

Hind tracks are 1-2 in. (3-5 cm) in length with 5 long toes.

bound

bound

Deer

Tracks are 2-3 in. (5-8 cm) long. Dew claws are evident in soft soil, snow and when running. A "pronk" is a trail left when the deer bounces forward with its front and rear hooves hitting the ground at the same time.

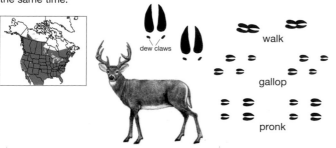

dew claws

walk

gallop

pronk

Elk

Tracks are 3.5-4.5 in. (9-11 cm) long. Other signs include antler rubs on small trees and wallows during mating season. Males are very vocal in the fall and bugle loudly to challenge other males.

walk

gallop

Pronghorn

Tracks are 2.5-3.5 in. (6-9 cm) long and wider at the base than those of deer. Dew claws are not evident.

amble

gallop

Bighorn Sheep

Tracks are 2.5-3.5 in. (6-9 cm) long. Hoof prints are splayed when running. Toes may be spread in front, making the tracks look square.

walk

Peccary (Javelina) & Wild Boar

Native collared peccaries (javelinas) have rounded tracks that are 1-2 in. (3-5 cm) long and lack dew claws. The introduced wild boar has tracks 2-3 in. (5-8 cm) long and prominent dew claws. Both leave similar trail patterns.

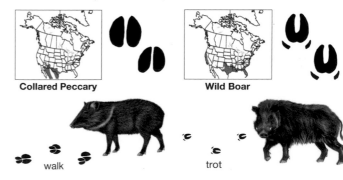

Collared Peccary

Wild Boar

walk

trot

36 37 38 39 40 41 42 43 44 45 46 47 48 49 50 51 52 53 54

15 16 17 18 19 20 21

Animals will see movement, patterns and abnormal shapes before they recognize you as an animal. Once they notice you, they'll see your eyes, face and hands, followed by the outline of your body. If you are tracking to hunt, cover your face and hands, and wear clothing that blends with the habitat around you. If you are tracking for either hunting or pleasure, be mindful of the impact of your activity. Trackers should respect the animal in its habitat to avoid disturbances which could cause them to abandon their nesting areas, leave their young, or leave their foraging areas. Frightening animals can cause flight that may injure them.

When you are tracking, the **landscape** will give you clues as to what you will find. Herbivores will seek refuge in a wide variety of vegetation including thick tangles, brush piles and rocks. They get water from dew and the plants they eat, so you may not necessarily find them near water. Certain animals, such as voles, rabbits and deer, are indicator species that will occur if the vegetation is good. And, in turn, they are prey for larger carnivores whose tracks you may see. Some habitats are better for tracking than others. Deep forests with light undergrowth don't offer enough good cover for most animals although you might see raccoons, rabbits and birds. In the same sense, fields offer little cover and so you'd only likely find trails on the field margins. The best area to look in is transition areas where there is a variety of vegetation and cover, and along water sources where larger mammals will drink.

Recognizing **travel routes** is another great way to find tracks. Animals will usually take the easiest route to travel, very much the way we use roads. The vegetation may be worn down or broken from frequent use by a variety of animals. Animal sleeping areas are another sign that wildlife is present. Beds can be found in a thick area of bush that offers the animal protection. Dens are usually underground, in rocks or built by the animals like beaver or rodents like chipmunks and squirrels.

An **animal's tracks**, one of the easiest signs to interpret, are defined by the shape of its feet, its weight, and the way it walks, runs or hops. The size of a track generally indicates the size of the animal. Sandy or muddy soils are the best places to find clear tracks.

While measurements given are of maximum sizes, they are intended to serve as general guidelines; keep in mind that tracks are influenced by several factors including the age and size of the animal, the material it walks on, the season (some mammals grow extra fur between their toes in winter), the age of the track and the animal's stride (is it walking, loping or running?).

When tracking:
1. Walk into the wind. Mammals have an excellent sense of smell and will leave an area once they pick up your scent.
2. Move slowly. Use binoculars to detect movement in the distance.
3. Be very quiet as you move. Advance a few steps at a time and avoid stepping on twigs.
4. Listen carefully for animals calling to each other or moving through the area.
5. Keep your distance. Move away from the animal if it stops feeding or appears nervous or startled.
6. Help protect threatened and endangered species by avoiding dens and nesting areas.
7. Obey all laws and ethical guidelines.

The **pattern of tracks** is also a good indicator of the species. Generally speaking, there are four kinds of track patterns. Deer, dog and cats are **diagonal walkers** and walk with a front foot and the opposite back foot moving at the same time. Most weasels are **bounders** and push off with their front feet, have their back feet land near the front feet tracks, and then push off with the back feet. Rabbits and most rodents are **gallopers** that push off with their back feet and land on their front feet with the front tracks behind the rear tracks. Lastly, raccoons, bears, porcupines and beavers are **amblers**, which move with a front foot and same side back foot moving at the same time.

TRACKS & TRAILS – 4 TOES

Coyotes & Foxes
Dog tracks show claws. The foot pad is small in relation to the toes and has a single lobe. They range in size from 2 in./5 cm long (kit fox) to 5 in./13 cm long (gray wolf). Wolves and coyotes are very vocal and make a variety of calls and choruses.

walk

lope

Bobcats & Cougars
Cat tracks do not show claws. The foot pad is large in relation to the toes and has two lobes. Note the rounded toe pads. They range in size from 2 in./5 cm long (bobcat) to 4 in./10 cm long (mountain lion).

walk

bound

Rabbits & Hares
Rabbits and hares all have rear feet at least twice as long as their front feet. When they bound, they land with their hind feet in front of their forefeet. As they speed up, their hind feet land further in front of their forefeet.

hop

jackrabbit gallop

TRACKS & TRAILS – 5 TOES

Bear
Bear tracks show claws. Human-like hind print ranges in size from 6 in./15 cm long (black bear) to 12 in./30 cm long (grizzly). Track is pigeon-toed. When the animal is ambling (a fast walk) the hind foot overtakes the front foot.

amble

gallop

Raccoon
Tracks are like small hands. Hind prints are 4 in. (10 cm) long and claws are clearly visible. Hips roll while walking causing the hind foot to register beside the opposite front foot.

walk

gallop

Opossum
Distinctive, hand-like tracks are about 2 in. (5 cm) wide. Tracks show tail dragging on ground between feet.

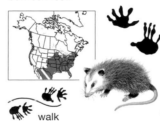

walk

Badger
Tracks are 2-3 in. (5-8 cm) long. Claw marks are longer on the fore print. Key signs are dens with large oval openings.

walk

Skunk
Hind print is 2-3 in. (5-8 cm) long; fore print is 1-2 in. (3-5 cm) long. Claws are often only evident on fore prints. Rotten egg smell is a key sign.

overstep walk

Common Muskrat
Hind track is about 3 in. (8 cm) long and has 5 toes. Leaves scat in piles near waterline. Look for floating grassy lodges near shore.

walk

TRACKS & TRAILS – 5 TOES

American Beaver
These animals have webbed feet. Hind tracks are about 6 in. (15 cm) long, and the webbing between the toes is often visible in mud.

walk

Nutria
This introduced and invasive animal has four visible front toes and webbing between 4 of the 5 toes on its hind feet. Tracks can be seen near slides, trails and exposed entrances to their burrows. A drag mark left by the tail may be seen between the footprints.

Northern River Otter
Otter's spreading tracks are about 3 in. (8 cm) across, and claws are visible. Webbing between the back toes is often evident in mud.

walk

TRACKS & TRAILS – 4 TOES & 5 TOES

Prairie Dog
Hind tracks are about 1.5 in. (4 cm) long with 5 toes. Front tracks show 4 toes.

walk

Norway Rat
Hind tracks show 5 toes and are 1.5-2.5 in. (4-6 cm) long. Front tracks show 4 toes and are about 1 in. (3 cm) long. Tracks in soft soil usually show tail drag between feet.

walk

Deer Mouse
Hind track is about .7 in. (1.8 cm) long. Front track shows 4 toes. Tracks in soft soil usually show tail drag between feet.

walk

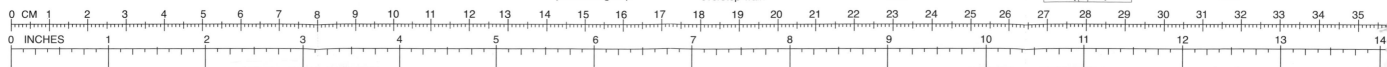